BIG Thoughts for Little Thinkers

BiG Thoughts for Little Thinkers

THE MISSION

BY JOEY ALLEN

New Leaf Press
A Division of New Leaf Publishing Group

First Printing: March 2005
Eighth Printing: November 2020

New Leaf Press Inc., PO Box 726, Green Forest, AR 72638

New Leaf Press is a division of the New Leaf Publishing Group, Inc.

Illustrations and text by Joey Allen

Please consider requesting that a copy of this volume be purchased by your local library system.

For my sister Bethany

ISBN-13: 978-0-89221-616-1
ISBN-13: 978-1-61458-148-2 (digital)
Library of Congress Control Number: 2004118192

Printed in China

Please visit our website for other great titles:
www.newleafpress.net

For information regarding author interviews,
please contact the publicity department at (870) 438-5288.

FOREWORD

Having five small grandchildren, I affirm the importance of influencing children with regard to missions at an early age. One cannot grow and mature in the Christian life without an understanding of and a commitment to our Great Commission task. One's understanding of salvation is deficient if it does not result in a desire to see a lost world come to faith in Jesus Christ. We are all naturally provincial in our perspective of the world. Consequently, it is important to cultivate in young children not only a God-consciousness and a love for Jesus but also an awareness of God's love for all people.

Joey Allen's book on missions in this series plants the seed for children to understand that missions outreach is a vital part of being a Christian. Properly nurtured, the concepts introduced in the following pages can inspire children to witness to others, to pray for the nations, and to understand what "God so loved the world" really means. May these truths prepare young, impressionable hearts to respond to God's call to reach the world for Christ.

– Jerry Rankin, President
International Mission Board, SBC

A WORD TO PARENTS AND TEACHERS

The *Big Thoughts for Little Thinkers* series was born out of the conviction that children need to be exposed to systematic theology from an early age. Moses instructed the people of Israel, "Impress [God's commandments] on your children. Talk about them when you sit at home and when you walk along the road, when you lie down and when you get up" (Deuteronomy 6:7). A foundation in theology enables our children to relate properly to God and His world.

Since the beginning of time, God's plan has been to redeem people from every nation, people who will revel and rejoice in an intimate relationship with Him. Against the onslaught of the world's confusing and conflicting messages, God's mission, His global and historic purpose, gives direction and clarity to our lives. God calls His children to rise above materialism and temporal pleasures in order to participate in His mission, the great adventure. How the mission is carried out varies for each of God's children, but participation is not optional — no matter how young in the faith.

This book is a tool that can help kindle in children a passion for God and a passion to see other people come to know and love Him. Ask your children diagnostic questions, assess their level of understanding, and take time to explain difficult concepts. May this book be a first step in challenging the next generation to spread the glory of God to the ends of the earth.

– Joey Allen

Hi! My name is Mikey. I want to tell you about God's mission.

God is at work in the world spreading His love and bringing people close to Him. You can be part of God's work in the world, too. This is what God's mission is all about.

John 5:17; 2 Corinthians 5:19

No one else is like God. God is so wonderful! Just think of all the things He has made — like bugs and raccoons and frogs and baboons! God wants everyone to know how wonderful He is.

Exodus 15:11; Isaiah 40:18–41:1

God loves the whole world. God wants people to be happy by being with Him. Real happiness only comes from God.

Psalm 16:11;
Jeremiah 29:11;
Philippians 4:4

When people try to find happiness without God, they do bad things called "sin." Sin makes God sad because it separates us from Him.

Ezekiel 18:4; Romans 3:23

Sin has messed up everything. Sin is the reason people fight and yell and hurt each other.

Genesis 3:14-19; Romans 3:10-18

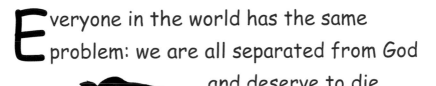

Everyone in the world has the same problem: we are all separated from God and deserve to die because of our sin. Have you ever been separated from your parents in a store? It is very scary.

Isaiah 59:2; Romans 6:23

But just like your parents look for you when you are separated from them, God looks for people who are separated from Him.

Luke 15; 19:10

God has a plan to fix everything. He could have fixed things by himself, but He loves to use people as part of His plan.

Genesis 12:1-3

*G*od sends people all over the world to tell others about Him. These people are called "missionaries."

Acts 1:8; 10:42; John 4:23

The whole Bible tells the story of God's mission. Many Bible characters like Abraham, Ruth, and Jonah were a part of God's mission. God sent messengers to show people His love.

Genesis 12; Ruth; Jonah

God even sent His very own Son Jesus on a mission to the earth. Jesus was on a special mission to bring people back to God.

Luke 19:10; 1 John 4:14

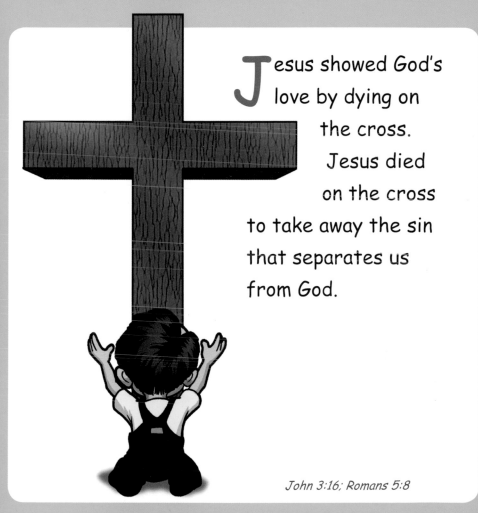

Jesus showed God's love by dying on the cross. Jesus died on the cross to take away the sin that separates us from God.

John 3:16; Romans 5:8

Jesus did what no one else could do. After He died on the cross, He rose from the dead and then went up to heaven. Now everyone who trusts in Jesus can go to heaven, too. This is the best news in the whole world!

Mark 16:6; 1 Corinthians 15:3–7

One day, there is going to be a huge party in heaven. People will be there from all over the world. Everyone will be singing and dancing and praising God.

Habakkuk 2:14;
Philippians 2:10–11;
Revelation 5:9

Everyone is invited to trust in Jesus. Some people will not trust in Jesus, but many people have never even heard of Him.

Romans 10:13; 1 John 2:2

Jesus is the only way to heaven, but people cannot trust in Jesus unless someone tells them about Him.

Acts 4:12; Romans 10:14-15

So many people need Jesus, but there are not many messengers. God wants to use you to tell other people about Jesus and invite them to the party in heaven. You can be one of God's messengers!

Matthew 9:37–38;
2 Timothy 4:5

Isn't it fun to help your mom bake a cake or help your dad fix the car? You can help God tell people the good news about Jesus.

1 Corinthians 3:9

The happiness God gives you makes you want to tell other people about Him. When you know how wonderful Jesus is, you want everyone to know Him!

Romans 10:1

God has a big job for us to do. God has told us to go to all the world and tell people about Him. Jesus is not just for people in America. He is for people in Africa, Asia, and Australia, too!

Isaiah 11:9; Ephesians 2:10

Even if you are a little kid, God can use you. God has given you special talents and abilities. He wants you to use them to show others how great He is.

Romans 12:4–8;
1 Corinthians 12:4–11;
1 Peter 4:10–11

You can be part of God's mission by telling your friends about Jesus. You don't have to be afraid to talk about Jesus. He promised that He would be with you and give you special help when you talk about Him.

Matthew 28:19-20

Learn more about God and His Word so you can share God's love with other people. Pray for people who have never heard about Jesus.

Ephesians 6:19-20; Colossians 4:3; 2 Thessalonians 3:1

You can help missionaries in other countries by praying for them, writing them letters or e-mails, or sending them presents.

Hebrews 6:10; 3 John 8

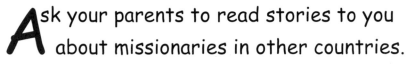
Ask your parents to read stories to you about missionaries in other countries. People in other countries sometimes look

different, talk different, and eat different things. It's fun to learn about what God is doing all over the world!

Thank you for letting me tell you about God's mission. I hope that you join Him in spreading the message of Jesus and His love around the world.

Also available in this series:

ISBN: 978-0-89221-614-7

ISBN: 978-0-89221-617-8

ISBN: 978-0-89221-615-4

Available at Christian bookstores nationwide

Big Thoughts for Little Thinkers

Big Thoughts for Little Thinkers